PICTURE LIBRARY

POLAR LANDS

PICTURE LIBRARY

POLAR LANDS

Norman Barrett

Franklin Watts

London   New York   Sydney   Toronto

© 1989 Franklin Watts

First published in the USA by
Franklin Watts Inc
387 Park Avenue South
New York
NY 10016

US ISBN: 0-531-10839-2
Library of Congress Catalog Card
Number 89-31504

Printed in Italy

Designed by
Barrett and Weintroub

Photographs by
GeoScience Features
Remote Source
Royal Geographical Society
Survival Anglia
N.S. Barrett Collection
Swedish National Tourist Office
Tourism Canada

Illustration by
Rhoda and Robert Burns

Technical Consultant
Keith Lye

Contents

Introduction

The polar lands are the regions around the earth's North and South Poles. They are cold, desolate areas, covered in ice and snow for all or most of the year.

The North Pole is a mostly ice-covered sea, the Arctic Ocean, surrounded by land. The South Pole is a frozen continent, Antarctica, surrounded by seas. Despite the harsh conditions, some plants grow in the polar lands and animals and even people live there.

△ An Eskimo village on the Arctic coast of Greenland. The Eskimos, who are also found in North America, live by hunting and fishing. Many now live in modern houses and use transportation such as helicopters and snowmobiles.

6

The lands that surround the Arctic Ocean include Canada, Alaska, the Soviet Union, Scandinavia and a large ice-covered island called Greenland. Many important air routes cross the Arctic, and the defenses of the world's great powers face each other across the ocean.

Antarctica is a huge frozen wilderness larger than Europe. But the seas around it and some coastal areas are rich in animal life.

△ The only people who brave Antarctica's harsh climate are scientists and explorers. Large colonies of penguins live on the coasts.

7

The lands around the poles

North polar region

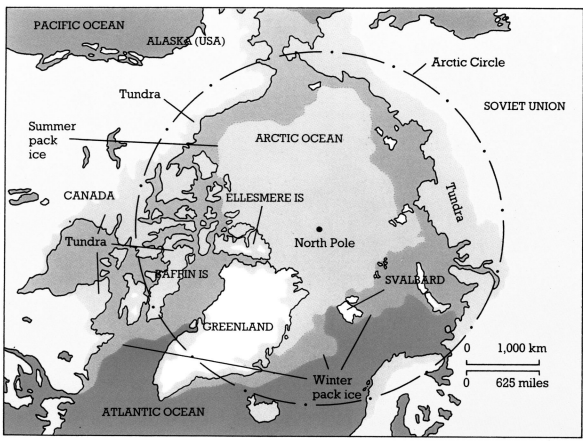

PACIFIC OCEAN
ALASKA (USA)
Arctic Circle
Tundra
SOVIET UNION
Summer pack ice
ARCTIC OCEAN
CANADA
ELLESMERE IS
Tundra
Tundra
North Pole
BAFFIN IS
SVALBARD
GREENLAND
Winter pack ice

0   1,000 km
0   625 miles

ATLANTIC OCEAN

Lands of the midnight sun

Because of the tilt of the earth's axis as it revolves around the sun, there are periods during the year when the sun does not set in the lands around the poles. These lands, within the Arctic and Antarctic Circles, are known as the lands of the midnight sun.

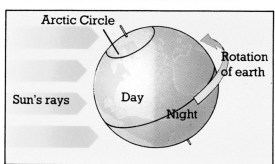

Arctic Circle
Rotation of earth
Sun's rays
Day
Night

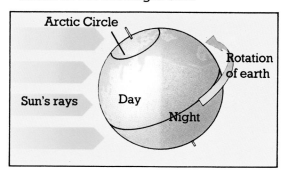

Arctic Circle
Rotation of earth
Sun's rays
Day
Night

South polar region

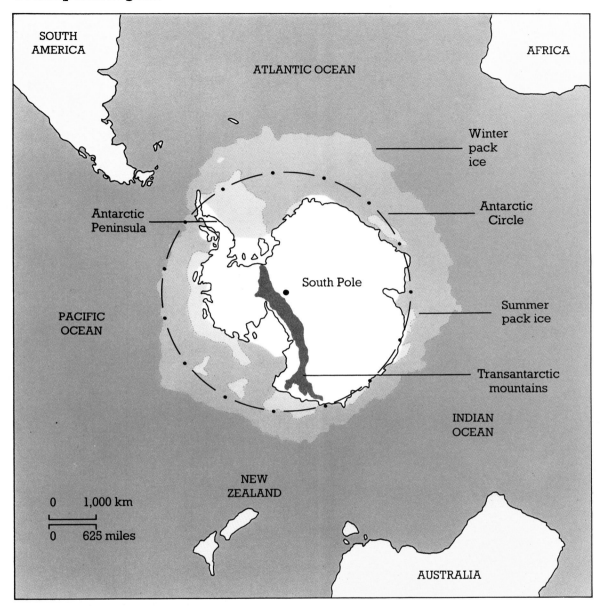

SOUTH
AMERICA

ATLANTIC OCEAN

AFRICA

Winter
pack
ice

Antarctic
Circle

Antarctic
Peninsula

South Pole

Summer
pack ice

PACIFIC
OCEAN

Transantarctic
mountains

INDIAN
OCEAN

0   1,000 km

0   625 miles

NEW
ZEALAND

AUSTRALIA

Loss of heat at the poles

The sun's rays lose heat as they travel
through the earth's atmosphere. More
heat is lost at the polar regions because
the rays enter the atmosphere at an
angle and have farther to travel. The
heat that gets through is also spread
over a much larger area near the poles
than in the regions around the equator.

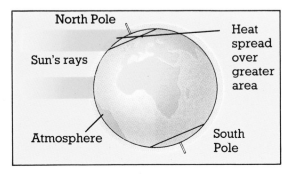

North Pole

Heat
spread
over
greater
area

Sun's rays

Atmosphere

South
Pole

Why it is cold at the poles

The polar regions are cold because of the way the earth moves around the sun. The sun's rays enter the earth's atmosphere at an angle near the poles, so much of the sun's heat is absorbed by the atmosphere.

The rays that get through to the polar regions are very weak. In the short summers, the sun is not strong enough to melt the great thickness of ice at the poles.

▽ The sun shines over the Antarctic, but the rays are weak. Even in midsummer, temperatures inland are several degrees below freezing point.

The tilt of the spinning earth as it moves around the sun affects the seasons in the polar regions. For half of each year, one pole is tilted away from the sun while the other pole is tilted toward it.

At the poles themselves, this means that there is continuous daylight for six months followed by six months of continuous night.

Away from the poles the periods of continuous night or day get shorter.

△ It is midnight in the Arctic, yet the sun shines on the icebergs floating off the Greenland coast. Places on or inside the Arctic and Antarctic circles are sometimes called the "lands of the midnight sun."

The Arctic Circle

Part of the Arctic Ocean is frozen throughout the year. Some of it freezes over only in winter.

Most of the ice on the ocean is sea ice. In autumn, fine crystals of ice begin to form. These increase to form a "sludge," which can freeze overnight to thick "pack ice."

Freshwater ice floating in the ocean includes huge icebergs, broken off from glaciers, and vast slabs of ice from Ellesmere Island.

△ A bay in Greenland begins to fill with pack ice. Icebergs can be seen in the background floating in the water, having broken off the mountain glaciers.

▷ Members of an expedition on the Arctic island of Svalbard explore a crevasse, a deep crack in a glacier.

▽ Icebergs floating in Arctic waters. Much more of an iceberg is below the water than above it. Only about an eighth to a tenth can be seen above the surface.

In some of the lands bordering the Arctic Ocean are low, treeless plains called tundra. Here, the ground is permanently frozen to a great depth except for a thin layer on top.

This top layer of soil thaws in the short spring and summer, and rich plant life appears. Flowers spring up and mosses and lichens reappear.

△ Mosses and lichens cover the ground in the short summer of Greenland's tundra regions.

▷ Most of Greenland is covered by a permanent icecap surrounded by coastal mountains, whose peaks jut through the ice.

The Antarctic

The Antarctic region contains the continent of Antarctica and the seas and oceans around it. The oceans are the southern parts of the Atlantic, Pacific and Indian Oceans. These waters are sometimes called the Antarctic Ocean.

The continent is covered by snow and ice, which in places is several miles thick. It has mountains, including an active volcano, and enormous ice shelves, slabs of ice that float onto the sea.

△ Explorers on the great icy wastes of Antarctica have to contend with the harshest conditions on earth. The central polar region is a high, flat plateau, where fierce winds blow and the world's coldest temperatures have been recorded.

▷ An icebreaker cuts through the frozen Antarctic Ocean.

◁ Some ice on the Antarctic Peninsula is colored pink by algae growing there. Except for birds and sea mammals on the coasts, there is very little life on Antarctica. Some lower forms of animal life, such as mites, can exist, but are active only in the summer. Only two kinds of flowering plants have been found.

▽ The peaks of the Transantarctic Mountains rise above the polar plateau.

The Antarctic icecap is so thick that the average height of the continent above sea level is about 2,300 m (7,500 ft). Mountain ranges stretch for 3,200 km (2,000 miles), dividing the continent into east and west. The Antarctic Peninsula extends for 1,300 km (800 miles) toward South America.

Antarctica is the windiest place on earth. Ferocious blizzards cover anything on the ground in huge snowdrifts.

Life in polar lands

The largest land animal in either polar region is the polar bear, which lives on the snow and ice of the Arctic. Mammals that live in the Arctic tundra include caribou, hares and foxes, and there are also owls and grouse.

Several kinds of whales and seals are found in the polar seas, and some species appear in both regions. Most polar mammals have thick fur or layers of fat to keep them warm.

△ Polar bear cubs stay with their mother until they are old enough to hunt for themselves. Polar bears roam the snowfields and float on ice. They are good swimmers. They feed mainly on seals and fish, but enjoy the plants of the tundra in the short Arctic summer.

Few species of animals live in the Antarctic region, but the bird and sea mammal populations are large. They are found in the seas and along the coasts.

Several kinds of penguins live in the Antarctic Ocean. They feed mainly on fish. They come ashore to nest and breed on Antarctica.

Whales and some seals live on tiny forms of sea life. Other seals eat crabs and fish, and the leopard seal also feeds on penguins.

▽ Emperor penguins are the largest species of penguin. They stand as high as 1.2 m (4 ft). Penguins cannot fly. They are fast underwater swimmers and spend most of their lives in the sea.

People have lived in the Arctic lands for thousands of years. The Eskimos live in the northern parts of Canada, Alaska, Greenland and the Soviet Union. The Lapps live in northern Scandinavia.

Eskimos have lived chiefly by hunting and fishing. But in more recent years, they have adapted their way of life to modern technology.

△ An Arctic fox, still in its white winter coat, enjoys the warmth of the tundra at the start of the short summer. During the summer, its fur turns brown or gray. Arctic foxes feed on small mammals or the remains of animals killed by polar bears.

▷ An Eskimo girl fishing through a hole in the ice and snow of Canada's Northwest Territories.

▽ Eskimo hunters shooting at seals from a boat. Not so long ago, they would have been using spears from a kayak, or canoe, as was their custom for thousands of years.

Research in polar lands

The polar lands are the last great regions on earth to be explored and studied. Research stations and weather observatories have been established in both areas.

Research has unearthed valuable deposits of minerals. Alaska is an important oil producer, and coal is mined on Svalbard. Lead and zinc are mined in Greenland. Antarctica is also rich in minerals.

△ A snowblower clears an ice road at the U.S. McMurdo Station, the largest research base on Antarctica.

Antarctica is of particular interest to scientists. Its weather and the oceans surrounding the continent are largely isolated from the rest of the world. This has helped to protect it from much pollution.

Several countries have scientific bases on Antarctica. Their studies include the upper atmosphere, weather, biology and many earth sciences.

▽ Scientists carry out a controlled explosion in the Antarctic ice. Such experiments provide information about the thickness of the ice and what lies under the icecap.

The future of polar lands

The lands of the Arctic belong to various nations and it is largely up to them how they are used. But there are international agreements that regulate fishing and whaling in Arctic waters.

Several countries have claims on different parts of Antarctica. Treaties have been signed by these nations and by others with scientific interest in the area. They set out rules for the use and conservation of the continent.

△ Seals, penguins and icebergs in the Antarctic. The relationship between the ocean wildlife and their environment is delicately balanced in the polar regions. Interference by humans or pollution from any source could seriously affect it.

The Antarctic treaties prohibit all military activity, nuclear explosions and disposal of radioactive waste. They encourage scientific investigation and cooperation between nations.

The establishment of Antarctica as a World Park under the United Nations has been proposed. The idea is to control all human activities and give maximum protection to the land and the wildlife in the oceans.

▽ A curious effect may be seen in the polar regions. Light reflected from tiny ice crystals in the clear air produces an image of the sun with a halo around it. It looks like a hole in the sky.

Unfortunately, a real hole in the atmosphere over Antarctica has been created by the use of certain aerosol sprays in the rest of the world. Gases from these sprays have damaged the protective ozone layer.

The story of polar lands

The Ice Ages

The earth was not always the way it is now. Millions of years ago, there were no ice sheets over the lands that now lie around the poles. It is thought that the polar lands once lay far away from the poles. They were then warm places with trees and plants. But the land areas have drifted toward the poles, and have gotten colder and colder as a result.

△ Dutch navigator Willem Barents became the first European to spend winter in the Arctic when his ship became icebound in 1596. He died on the return journey.

Over the last two million years, great areas of the earth have been periodically covered by ice. During these Ice Ages, ice sheets spread over large areas. In the last Ice Age, which ended only about 10,000 years ago, ice sheets spread as far south as New York and London.

Opening up the Arctic

In the late 800s, Vikings from Scandinavia began to colonize Iceland. But it was not for another 600 or 700 years, in the great age of discovery, that explorers became interested in the Arctic.

The lure that enticed adventurers into the freezing Arctic seas was to find a new route to the spices and treasures of the East.

In 1576, English navigator Martin Frobisher sailed around Greenland and discovered Frobisher Bay on Baffin Island, in Canada's northwest.

In 1596, the heroic Dutch sailor Willem Barents discovered West Spitzbergen, the largest island in the group now called Svalbard.

△ Roald Amundsen is photographed taking readings at the South Pole.

In 1741, Vitus Bering, a Dane in the service of the Russian Navy, sailed north along the coast of Siberia and discovered Alaska.

△ Inside the hut where Captain Scott made his headquarters before starting off on his fated expedition to the South Pole in 1911.

In 1831, British explorer James Clark Ross discovered the North Magnetic Pole, the place toward which compass needles point. He later led expeditions to the Antarctic and made important discoveries there.

These and other daring and courageous men paved the way for the explorers of the 1900s.

Race for the poles

The early 20th century was a time of adventure. The poles were the last of the world's places yet to be reached, and expeditions were set up to explore the regions.

Two Americans claimed to have discovered the North Pole, Dr. Frederick A. Cook in April 1908 and Robert E. Peary a year later. Peary's claim was eventually accepted, but there have been serious doubts since.

The South Pole was first reached in 1911 by Roald Amundsen of Norway. A month after Amundsen, the tragic British expedition led by Captain Robert Scott arrived at the Pole, only to perish on the way back.

Since those days, several expeditions have succeeded in reaching the South Pole. But life and travel are never easy on Antarctica, the world's "last great wilderness."

△ British explorers at the South Pole in 1986 after tracing the route of Captain Scott 75 years earlier. A striped pole topped with a globe marks the pole, and flags of other successful expeditions stand nearby.

Facts and records

△ Ice climbing in Antarctica. The continent contains about nine-tenths of the world's ice.

Driest place with most water!
Antarctica is a remarkable continent. It is the driest place on earth. Plenty of snow falls, but some parts of Antarctica have had no rain for two million years. Yet it contains about 70 percent of the world's fresh water.

The explanation of this oddity is that the water is in the form of ice. The great ice sheet that covers almost the whole continent to a great depth contains about 90 percent of the world's ice.

Coldest and windiest
Among the records Antarctica holds is that of the coldest place on earth. The lowest temperature ever recorded was −89°C (−128°F), at the Soviet base Vostok in July 1983. Gales of 320 km/h (200 mph) blow at Commonwealth Bay, making it the windiest place on earth, too.

Reaching the poles
The first person to reach the South Pole was Norwegian explorer Roald Amundsen, by dog-drawn sleds on December 16, 1911. The first to reach the North Pole on a solo journey was Japanese explorer Naomi Uemura, with a sled drawn by 17 huskies, on May 1, 1978.

Glossary

Algae
A group of simple plants without proper stems, roots or leaves.

Atmosphere
The envelope of air that surrounds the earth.

Crevasse
A deep crack in a glacier.

Environment
The external conditions that influence the life and development of people, animals and plants.

Glacier
A mass of ice that moves slowly under its own weight toward the sea.

Ice Ages
Periods of thousands of years when ice covered much greater areas of the earth than it does now.

Icecap
A mass of ice and snow covering a large area. The largest icecaps are called ice sheets.

Ice shelf
A vast body of ice that extends off the land over the sea.

Lichen
A group of plants that form tufts and crusts on stones and soil.

Ozone layer
A layer in the earth's upper atmosphere that contains most of the atmosphere's ozone, a form of oxygen. It absorbs some of the sun's burning rays. Without this protection, plants would die and people would receive harmful radiation.

Pack ice
Large blocks of ice floating on the sea formed by small pieces of ice joining together.

Plateau
A large, high area of level land.

Radioactive waste
Unwanted products from nuclear power stations that contain harmful radiation.

Snowmobile
A motorized sled.

Tundra
The low, treeless plains in some Arctic lands. They are mostly permanently frozen except for a thin top layer that thaws in the summer.

Index